The Storytellers

by Brian Way

First Produced by Theatre Centre Ltd.,
London, England in 1955.

Single copies of plays are sold for reading purposes only. The copying or duplicating of a play, or any part of play, by hand or by any other process, is an infringement of the copyright. Such infringement will be vigorously prosecuted.

Baker's Plays
7611 Sunset Blvd.
Los Angeles, CA 90042
bakersplays.com

NOTICE

This book is offered for sale at the price quoted only on the understanding that, if any additional copies of the whole or any part are necessary for its production, such additional copies will be purchased. The attention of all purchasers is directed to the following: this work is fully protected under the copyright laws of the United States of America, the British Commonwealth, including Canada, and all other countries of the Copyright Union. Violations of the Copyright Law are punishable by fine or imprisonment, or both. The copying or duplication of this work or any part of this work, by hand or by any process, is an infringement of the copyright and will be vigorously prosecuted.

This play may not be produced by amateurs or professionals for public or private performance without first submitting application for performing rights. Licensing fees are due on all performances whether for charity or gain, or whether admission is charged or not. Since performance of this play without the payment of the licensing fee renders anybody participating liable to severe penalties imposed by the law, anybody acting in this play should be sure, before doing so, that the licensing fee has been paid. Professional rights, reading rights, radio broadcasting, television and all mechanical rights, etc. are strictly reserved. Application for performing rights should be made directly to BAKER'S PLAYS.

No one shall commit or authorize any act or omission by which the copyright of, or the right to copyright, this play may be impaired. No one shall make any changes in this play for the purpose of production.

Publication of this play does not imply availability for performance. Both amateurs and professionals considering a production are strongly advised in their own interest to apply to Baker's Plays for written permission before starting rehearsals, advertising, or booking a theatre.

Whenever the play is produced, the author's name must be carried in all publicity, advertising and programs. Also, the following notice must appear on all printed programs, "Produced by special arrangement with Baker's Plays."

Licensing fees for THE STORYTELLERS are based on a per performance rate and payable one week in advance of the production.

Please consult the Baker's Plays website at www.bakersplays.com or our current print catalogue for up to date licensing fee information.

Copyright © 1977 by Brian Way
Made in U.S.A.
All rights reserved.

THE STORYTELLERS
ISBN **978-0-87440-605-4**
#1245-B

THE STORYTELLERS was first produced by Theatre Centre Ltd., London, England in 1955.

CONDITIONS FOR PERFORMANCE: This play is intended for presentation to family audiences and/or children 5—11 years of age. This play must be presented by adults (or young adults). Because of the participation, the audience may not exceed a maximum of 400 with proscenium staging, or a maximum of 300 with open staging (preferably with bleacher seating). ROYALTIES are due on all performances of Brian Way plays, whether admission is charged or not. Production fee on this title is as follows: $45.00 for the first performance and $35.00 for each subsequent performance.

PRINTED FORM: This large size play script is printed in such a manner for the convenience in making rehearsal notations.

CHARACTERS IN ORDER OF APPEARANCE

Toyman   Mirrorman

THE REAL PRINCESS

King   Page
Queen   Attendants
Prince   Princess
Lady-in-Waiting

THE GIANT WITH THE THREE GOLDEN HAIRS

Starlight   Queen
Edward   1st Guard
King   2nd Guard
Old Woman   3rd Guard
1st Robber   Giant's Grandmother
2nd Robber   The Giant
Other Robbers   Princess

THE ELVES AND THE SHOEMAKER

The Shoemaker   King of the Elves
His Wife   Elves

THE NIGHTINGALE

The Emperor   Courtier*
The Lord Chancellor   Kitchen Maid
1st Property Man   The Artificial Nightingale
2nd Property Man   The Wathmaker
The Nightingale   The Doctor

* This part may be made female.

A fantasy play which includes within an original setting adaptations of:

    The Real Pincess
        by Hans Anderson
    The Giant with the Three Golden Hairs
        by the Brothers Grimm
    The Elves and the Shoemaker
        by the Brothers Grimm
    The Nightengale
        by Hans Anderson

ACT I

SCENE. A Toyshop. In a prominent position there is a full-length "mirror." The TOYMAN is working; how he got into his shop without anyone seeing him is a mystery; some people may have seen him walk in, and if they have, then they will probably tell all the others: well, that's all right. The TOYMAN himself is really too busy to bother about them anyway. He is completing a new toy and he is gently tapping the last few nails with a hammer.

TOYMAN   One more! And then, I think, it's finished. Here goes, then. *(He taps the nail in, and then holds up the toy - it is a musical box.)* There we are - finished. And, my word, it looks nice. Very nice indeed. *(He looks up and notices audience.)* Oh, hello. I didn't see you come in. Hum! How jolly. Are - are you all right? All comfortable? Good, good. Well, it's very nice of you, I'm sure. Look - look what I've just finished making. I was just thinking that it's rather nice. D'you think so? Eh? Still, of course, that's only the outside, and it's not the looks that count. It's what's inside that's important. If that doesn't work, then the outside might as well be an old tin can. I'd better try it. Oh dear, what if it doesn't work. Same old trouble - every time I make a toy, I - I get nervous about trying it. In case it doesn't work. I know. I'll try it. It's the only way, isn't it? Here goes then. *(He opens the lid, and beautiful music comes from the box. He listens, happily tapping his foot, at the end of the melody, he closes the box and the music stops.)* Well, it does work. That's splendid. I am glad about that, you know. I've made it for the Princess, and she's such a difficult girl to please. I - I don't mean she's not nice, but - well, you see, being a princess, she has so many, many toys that it really is rather difficult to make something that she hasn't got. So what I did was this. I wrote to Her Majesty the Queen and asked what she thought the Princess would like. And I got a letter back a few days later, with a long list of things - and there was a little note attached saying: "Any one of these would be lovely" - signed "Queen." Well, it was still very difficult, so d'you know what I did? I got a pin, and held it in my hand like this - then I spun round and round and stuck the pin in the list. Like this. *(He does it.)* And there it was - a musical box. So I made it and here it is. And now I'll have to hope I've done the right thing. Anyway, it's too late now. Her birthday's tomorrow so I shall have to take it to the Palace today. In fact, I'd better take it now. No time like the present. I'll just have a little tidy up and go straight away.

(He goes to the long "mirror" in the workshop and starts to tidy himself. His reflection, i.e. The MIRRORMAN, should be dressed and made up in every detail as he is himself.)

(Talking to himself in the mirror.) Ooh! I don't look so bad. Smooth the hair down a bit - there. That's better. Straighten the neckerchief - so - and so. There. That's much better. Eyebrows - yes. Oh, dear. This mirror is dirty. (To us.*) Thought I'd got a dirty face for a moment. But it's all on the mirror. Can't have that. (Takes out handkerchief and cleans it.) There! There! That's a great improvement. Oh, what a lot of dust. (He sneezes - once - twice - and the third time stops it - but his reflection isn't in time to stop and does sneeze.) Ooh! That was funny. Did - did you notice anything? Eh? Did he sneeze when I didn't? I think he did, you know. How very odd. He can't do that sort of thing. It'll upset all the arrangements. Perhaps I imagined it. I know. (He winks at all of us, and then suddenly bobs down - then up again - then down - then very slowly up and bobs down. Then he pushes one finger up and draws a pattern on the mirror - but all this his reflection does perfectly with him.) Seems to be all right. How strange. (Suddenly he starts an energetic series of movements in all directions, which his reflection manages perfectly to begin with and then gets so worn out that he can't go on any more.)

MIRRORMAN   Stop! Stop!

TOYMAN   What d'you mean, "Stop?" You can't till I stop!

MIRRORMAN   I know. I know. But you can't expect me to go on bobbing up and down like that. I shall get tired out.

TOYMAN   What do you mean, "tired out?" Aren't you my reflection?

MIRRORMAN   Of course I am.

TOYMAN   Then you can't get tired out until I do.

MIRRORMAN   Well - aren't you tired?

TOYMAN   Yes. Yes, I am a bit.

MIRRORMAN   There you are then.

TOYMAN   But I'm getting very old, you know.

* See page 61.

MIRRORMAN	No older than I am.
TOYMAN	What? Oh! No, I suppose I'm not.
MIRRORMAN	Anyway, I wanted to have a chat with you.
TOYMAN	A chat?
MIRRORMAN	Yes.
TOYMAN	With me?
MIRRORMAN	Well, I couldn't talk to anyone else. Could I?
TOYMAN	No. I suppose not. Well, what was it about?
MIRRORMAN	I don't want anyone else to hear. It's private.
TOYMAN	Is it?
MIRRORMAN	Very much so.
TOYMAN	And secret too?
MIRRORMAN	Very secret.
TOYMAN	Oh!
MIRRORMAN	Is there anyone else about?
TOYMAN	Well - yes. Actually. Quite a lot of people.
MIRRORMAN	Oh, that's a pity.
TOYMAN	Perhaps you could whisper it.
MIRRORMAN	Yes, I could do that, couldn't I?
TOYMAN	*(To us.)* Excuse me. *(The MIRRORMAN whispers something.)* No! Really?
MIRRORMAN	Yes. Really. It's perfectly true. I heard her telling the King last night.
TOYMAN	Oh dear, oh dear. How awful! How dreadful! I say, I hope you won't mind - but I think I *ought* to tell these people. They ought to know about this. Do you mind?
MIRRORMAN	Well, no - as long as they keep it to themselves.
TOYMAN	Oh, I'm sure they will. *(To us.)* Do you know what he's just told me? It's most upsetting. Have you got any idea? *(Various answers may come.)* No - No -

it's not that. Oh, you'll never guess. It's this. My present for the Princess is no good. No good at all. He's just told me. He heard the Queen tell the King last night that somebody else has already sent a Musical Box. Yesterday! Oh dear, this is upsetting. *(To MIRRORMAN.)* You didn't by any chance hear what she would like? Not that it's any good asking - I haven't got time to make anything *now*. Not by tomorrow.

MIRRORMAN   Well, as a matter of fact, I did hear of one thing she hasn't got.

TOYMAN   Really? What was that?

MIRRORMAN   Storytellers!

TOYMAN   Storytellers! What d'you mean - storytellers?

MIRRORMAN   Well, just that - storytellers.

TOYMAN   Oh, I see. You mean - a - a story-book.

MIRRORMAN   No, no. Silly. If I meant a story-book, I'd say a story-book, I said storytellers.

TOYMAN   *(Moving away.)* Tut! Storytellers! Storytellers! Pooh! Just sounds like a lot of magic to me.

MIRRORMAN   That's right.

TOYMAN   What is?

MIRRORMAN   A lot of magic. The storytellers. It's magic.

TOYMAN   How d'you mean?

MIRRORMAN   Come back here and I'll tell you.

TOYMAN   Will you? *(Goes back.)* Well?

MIRRORMAN   Oh, dear. I can't tell you. I'll have to show you.

TOYMAN   Then go on - show me.

MIRRORMAN   I can't.

TOYMAN   Of course you can. I can see!

MIRRORMAN   Yes, yes. But I have to give you something.

TOYMAN   Give me something?

MIRRORMAN   Yes, to put in the box.

TOYMAN	Oh, I say. That is difficult isn't it?
MIRRORMAN	Very. Never mind. Let's try. I'll have to come through the mirror.
TOYMAN	Through the mirror?
MIRRORMAN	Yes.
TOYMAN	But you can't do that.
MIRRORMAN	Oh yes, I can. I think. Anyway, I can with a bit of help.
TOYMAN	What sort of help?
MIRRORMAN	Wait a minute. I'll look it up in the book. *(He produces an enormous book labelled simply "Instructions.")* Now, let's see. "Instructions for getting through mirrors - page one thousand two hundred and thirty-four." I know it's very difficult. Or I'd have tried it before. Ah! Here we are. Page 1234. "Instructions for getting through mirrors."
TOYMAN	What's it say?
MIRRORMAN	"Take more than three hundred voices" - *(Or two hundred, or one hundred, according to size of audience)* - "and make them go hum."
TOYMAN	Well I never.
MIRRORMAN	There's the snag, you see. I've never even seen three hundred voices. So I've never been able to do it.
TOYMAN	I see. Wait a minute, though. I've got an idea. Excuse me. *(To us.)* How many of you are there? How many? Goodness gracious. That's more than three hundred, isn't it? There you are, Mr. Mirrorman - more than three hundred voices.
MIRRORMAN	How wonderful! Will they help?
TOYMAN	Of course they will. What do they have to do?
MIRRORMAN	Hum! That's all. Hum. Oh no - wait a minute. It says a bit more here. "The voices must hum all together very gently or it won't work." There. Now, what about it?
TOYMAN	Well, let's try it. You get ready to come through. That's it. Now - the hum.

(The audience hums very gently. The MIRRORMAN feels the mirror all over - it is very hard. Gradually - very gradually, it gets softer, till first one finger, then a hand, another hand, an arm, both arms, slip through the mirror, and are followed by the rest of him. Finally he is through.)

TOYMAN   It's worked! It's worked! How wonderful!

MIRRORMAN   It is pretty good, isn't it? *(To us.)* Thanks very much.

TOYMAN   What's it feel like?

MIRRORMAN   I dunno. Hum. Treacle! Yes, that's it. Treacle.

TOYMAN   Well, how do you do? It's nice to meet you at last.

(They shake hands.)

MIRRORMAN   You too. I won't ask what you've been doing, 'cos I know.

TOYMAN   Do you?

MIRRORMAN   Well, I've been doing the same thing, silly.

TOYMAN   Of course you have. I was forgetting. Now - what about the storytellers?

MIRRORMAN   Here they are. In this packet.

TOYMAN   It's rather small, isn't it?

MIRRORMAN   Oh, it's big enough. Things don't always have to be big.

TOYMAN   No, I suppose not.

MIRRORMAN   Well. Aren't you going to open it?

TOYMAN   Oh yes. Of course. *(He does so.)* Here we are! Well, I never. A pea - a nail - a feather - and one, two - two golden hairs.

MIRRORMAN   Two? There ought to be three, all tied together.

TOYMAN   Ought there? Oh, yes. Here we are. Three golden hairs. Well, what on earth do I do with these?

MIRRORMAN   Put them in the musical box.

TOYMAN   All right. *(He does so.)* Now what?

MIRRORMAN	Send it to the Princess.
TOYMAN	What! Just like that?
MIRRORMAN	Yes.
TOYMAN	Well, I must say I don't see anything particularly special about that.
MIRRORMAN	Don't you? Oh, no wait. I nearly forgot the most important bit. The instructions. You must put these in as well.
TOYMAN	*(Reading.)* "Sleep with one of these under your pillow and you will dream a different story every night." Well, I never. How amazing!
MIRRORMAN	Yes, isn't it?
TOYMAN	What sort of stories?
MIRRORMAN	Oh, all sorts.
TOYMAN	Can I hear them?
MIRRORMAN	Oh no, they're not to be heard. You see them.
TOYMAN	Really! Can I see them?
MIRRORMAN	If you sleep with the things under your pillow.
TOYMAN	But I can't do that. I've got to take them to the Princess. Oh, what a shame! I should like to have seen them.
MIRRORMAN	Well, you could, of course, see them all now.
TOYMAN	Where?
MIRRORMAN	On the other side of the mirror - in mirrorland.
TOYMAN	Do you mean to say you have them there?
MIRRORMAN	Oh yes. They're going on all the time *there*. All you'd have to do would be to hold the things in your hand.
TOYMAN	All at once.
MIRRORMAN	No, no. One at a time. Then you'd see the stories one at a time.
TOYMAN	How wonderful.

MIRRORMAN   Which first?

TOYMAN   Er - the pea.

MIRRORMAN   All right. Come with me.

TOYMAN   Do you think I can get through as well?

MIRRORMAN   Of course you can. As long as more than three hundred voices hum. Now - stand still - feel the mirror - now the hum.

(And with the humming they go through. Once they are through another sound starts.)

MIRRORMAN   Listen! *(Royal Procession music is heard.)* It's the procession. Quick! Over here.

(Before moving, the TOYMAN changes the "Mirror" into a throne. They go somewhere to sit - possibly with the audience.)

THE REAL PRINCESS

(The procession consists of the KING, the QUEEN, the LADY-IN-WAITING, the PAGE, and the PRINCE. The KING and QUEEN sit on their thrones.)

KING   Welcome home, my boy. Messenger!

PAGE   Your Majesty.

KING   Let it be declared throughout all my Kingdom that my son, the Royal Prince, has returned from his journey and that therefore tomorrow shall be a holiday.

PAGE   Yes, your Majesty. *(He goes.)*

QUEEN   Welcome home, my son.

PRINCE   Thank you, my Royal mother and father.

QUEEN   We shall have a great feast, and after you have eaten and rested you must tell us about your travels.

PRINCE   Oh, mother. I have such a story to tell that it would fill a hundred books and take a hundred men a hundred days to write them. And I have returned with great riches such as your kingdom has never seen. And I have found -

KING   A Princess?

PRINCE	No, Royal father. I have not found a Princess.
KING	None at all?
PRINCE	Oh, I have seen many - one for each day of the year I have been away.
KING	Three hundred and sixty-five princesses!
QUEEN	It was a leap year, my dear.
KING	So it was. I beg your pardon. Three hundred and sixty-six princesses - and you have returned without one of them. Indeed?
PRINCE	My Royal father - none of them was a *real* Princess.
KING	Pooh! Methinks you're too fussy.
PRINCE	But surely, no. One day the Princess and I will be King and Queen - and only the best will do for this Kingdom.
KING	Yes, true. But everybody has a few faults - even Princesses.
QUEEN	Quite right, my son. We cannot be too careful. The right one is sure to come along one day.

(Enter PAGE.)

KING	Well?
PAGE	Your Majesty, there is a girl at the gate.
KING	A girl? What sort of a girl?
PAGE	She says she is a Princess, your Majesty.
KING	Well, if she says she is, perhaps she is, and if she is, she'll be very welcome I'm sure. Show her in.
PAGE	Yes, your Majesty.
KING	And let the trumpets sound a fanfare.

(The trumpets sound a fanfare. A somewhat bedraggled women enters alone, goes straight to the throne and curtseys.)

KING	Welcome to you, my child. What is your business?
PRINCESS	Your Royal Majesties, I have heard tell that your

	Royal son, the Prince, seeks a bride. I have journeyed for many months to offer him my hand.
PRINCE	Your hand? But it's not a Royal hand. You aren't a real Princess.
PRINCESS	I most certainly am.
PRINCE	But your clothes are all torn -
QUEEN	And your crown's awry -
KING	And you have no shoes -
PRINCE	And where are your ladies-in-waiting? -
QUEEN	And your dowry of silver and gold? -
KING	And your horses?
PRINCE	And servants?
KING and QUEEN	And -
PRINCE	And everything else to prove you're a real Princess?
PRINCESS	Your Majesties, in my journey to your kingdom I was shipwrecked on the stormy seas and lost all of these things -
KING	All of them?
PRINCESS	All of them, your Majesties. I possess nothing but the dress in which I stand.
KING	How sad. How very sad.
LADY-IN-WAITING	How careless.
QUEEN	You poor unfortunate girl.
LADY-IN-WAITING	Beware, your Majesties. How do we know that this is not some servant girl tricking her way to your Kingdom?
KING	No! That is a terrible thought.
QUEEN	Surely no one would dare -
KING	Exactly! No one would dare to trick the King.
QUEEN	Or the Queen.

PRINCE	They might. How do we know?
PRINCESS	You are right to be so careful, your Royal Majesties -
LADY-IN-WAITING	Your Majesties? May I make a suggestion?
KING	You may.
LADY-IN-WAITING	Why not put the girl to some test?
KING	A test?
LADY-IN-WAITING	Yes, your Majesty - then she can *prove* her story that she is a real princess.
KING	What a good idea.
QUEEN	The very thing.
KING	We'll put her to a test.
PRINCE	What test, your Majesty?
KING	What test? Well, I haven't thought of that. Have you an idea?
LADY-IN-WAITING	No, your Majesty. I'm afraid I haven't.
KING	What about you, my boy?
PRINCE	I don't know of one either.
KING	It really is very difficult.
QUEEN	I know. I can think of a test.
KING	How clever you are, my Queen.
QUEEN	Let this girl be taken to the Royal kitchens and given something to eat. Whilst she's away we'll devise the test.
KING	*(To PRINCESS.)* My dear I hope you don't think this very rude of us. We really must be certain.
PRINCESS	Of course, your Majesty. I quite understand.
KING	Page! Conduct the Princess - the lady - to the Royal kitchen.
PAGE	Yes, your Majesty.

(They go.)

KING	Now we are alone, tell us your idea, my Queen.
QUEEN	Well - let us allow this girl to sleep in the bed reserved for Royal guests - but, let us place on the bed twenty mattresses and on top of those twenty feather beds.
KING	Twenty mattresses?
PRINCE	Why?
QUEEN	Wait. I haven't finished yet. When all are piled high - making the softest bed in all the world - let us place at the very bottom, underneath the twenty feather beds and the twenty mattresses - let us place -
KING	What?
PRINCE	What?
QUEEN	*A pea!*
KING	A pea?
PRINCE	A pea?
LADY-IN-WAITING	A pea?
KING	An ordinary pea?
PRINCE	From a sack in the Royal kitchen?
QUEEN	That's right. An ordinary pea from the sack in the Royal kitchen.
KING and PRINCE	But why?
QUEEN	Because, if the girl is a *real* princess, she won't sleep a wink all night. She'll be so uncomfortable and twist and turn, and cover herself with bruises. Anyone else wouldn't notice a thing - but a *real* princess couldn't sleep.
KING	What a splendid idea!
PRINCE	A wonderful idea!
KING	We must go at once and prepare the bed.
QUEEN	We'll ask some of the Royal servants to help us.

(Improvised sequence in which the PRINCE and the QUEEN and the LADY-IN-WAITING get the audience (two or four at a time) to pile twenty mattresses and twenty feather beds under supervision of the KING, who merrily counts them. When all is done -).

KING 'Tis done. 'Tis done. Thank you, Royal servants. And now my dear, the pea.

QUEEN Oh dear. I've lost it. Where on earth can I have put it?

MIRRORMAN *(To TOYMAN.)* Go on. Give it to her.

TOYMAN Me?

MIRRORMAN Yes. Quickly.

TOYMAN Your Majesty. The pea.

QUEEN Oh, thank you, Royal Toyman. Here it is, your Majesty.

KING Give it to our son. *(She does so.)* Now, my boy, push it under the pile - right to the very middle. *(The PRINCE does so.)* Now, let us all go to bed. We'll send the Lady-in-waiting to tell the girl -

QUEEN Yes, what shall we tell her?

KING That the test will happen tomorrow. Go, Lady-in-waiting. Summon the girl to bed.

LADY-IN-WAITING Yes, your Majesty. *(She goes.)*

KING Come, my dear. And you my son. Tomorrow morning we'll know the truth.

(They go. Enter the PRINCESS alone.)

PRINCESS What strange people they are. Still - they're rather nice and their idea of having a test is only to be expected. But I do wish I didn't have to wait until tomorrow. *(She yawns.)* Ahh! I'm so tired. I'm really glad to go to bed. A good night's sleep and I shall pass the test easily.

(She gets into bed. Lies down. At once she is most uncomfortable. She twists and turns and moans and groans, bashes the bed and scratches her head, but all to no avail. She just cannot sleep. Suddenly she leaps out of bed -)

PRINCESS   I won't stand it another minute. What an insult!
                  How could anyone sleep in a bed with a lump in it?
                  Your Majesty. Your Majesty! *(To us.)* Do please
                  call him for me. *(All.)* Your Majesty.

(Enter KING, PRINCE, QUEEN.)

KING   What on earth is the matter?

PRINCESS   The matter? The matter, your Majesty, is with the
                  bed. There's something dreadfully hard in it. I
                  can't possibly sleep, and I'm bruised black and blue
                  from head to toe.

QUEEN   Then she must be real -

KING   She must be real -

PRINCE   A Real Princess - at last!

(Music.)

KING   Tell all my Kingdom that tomorrow shall be a Royal
                  Holiday for the Royal Wedding.

(Procession out.)

MIRRORMAN   Quick. Quick. Go and fetch it.

TOYMAN   What?

MIRRORMAN   The pea, of course.

TOYMAN   Oh yes, of course. *(He retrieves the pea.)* I say,
                  that was rather nice. I enjoyed it very much.

MIRRORMAN   I thought you would.

TOYMAN   And will *our* Princess see that story if she sleeps
                  with the pea under her pillow?

MIRRORMAN   Of course she will - exactly as we saw it.

TOYMAN   Well, I never. That's lovely. Now what am I going
                  to see?

MIRRORMAN   It depends what you have in your hand next.

TOYMAN   Let me see. It's the three golden hairs.

MIRRORMAN   Then it'll be that story. *(The TOYMAN changes the
                  "throne" into a wall.)*

TOYMAN   Whose hairs are they?

MIRRORMAN	You'll see in time. I'm not going to tell you *all* the story.
TOYMAN	Oh, are you going to tell *any* of it?
MIRRORMAN	The first part, yes, because that happened many years ago. Now, hold the hairs very tightly in your hand -
TOYMAN	Why?
MIRRORMAN	I can't start the story unless you do. You see, if you hold them very tightly, then music will start - and once the music starts the whole story will come back to me -
TOYMAN	Oh, I see. Right. I'm holding them very tightly.
MIRRORMAN	A bit tighter still.
TOYMAN	Like that?
MIRRORMAN	That's better. Listen!

(*Music starts. Both men are very still, the MIRRORMAN drawing inspiration from the music. At last he starts his story.*)

THE GIANT WITH THE THREE GOLDEN HAIRS

MIRRORMAN	Once upon a time there was a poor man who had a son. The baby was born under a lucky star - look, there it is. (*The star drops out of the sky.*) And the fortune-tellers told the poor man that when his son grew up he would marry the King's daughter. But it so happened that one day the King, in disguise, passed through the village where the poor man and his son lived. And the king asked the people if there was any news. "Oh yes," the people said, "a child has been born under that lucky star, and when he grows up he's going to marry the King's daughter."
TOYMAN	Did they know it was the King?
MIRRORMAN	No, I told you. He was in disguise.
TOYMAN	Oh yes. Sorry. I won't interrupt any more.
MIRRORMAN	Well, the King wasn't a bit pleased about this, so he went to the child's parents and asked them to sell him their son. They didn't want to, of course, but the King offered a whole sack of gold, and as they didn't have any bread to eat, and hadn't enough money to look after the baby properly, they finally agreed. And they remembered something else as well. Guess what?

TOYMAN   What?

MIRRORMAN   No, you must guess.

TOYMAN   Hum. I know - they remembered the lucky star.

MIRRORMAN   Exactly. They remembered the lucky star and so knew that no harm could come to their son. Well, the king put the child into a box and rode away. But when he came to a deep stream he threw the child into it and thought to himself: "There. That's that. That young gentleman will never be my daughter's husband."

TOYMAN   Did the box sink?

MIRRORMAN   You'll see. Don't keep interrupting.

TOYMAN   Sorry.

MIRRORMAN   No, it didn't sink. It floated down the stream, watched over carefully by Starlight - look, there she is.

(STARLIGHT appears under the star.)

TOYMAN   Starlight?

MIRRORMAN   That's right. The spirit from the star. Try and catch her!

TOYMAN   Me?

MIRRORMAN   Yes. Go on.

TOYMAN   All right. (He creeps slowly up behind STARLIGHT - suddenly she swishes round and, with a strange sound and a quick movement of her arms, puts a spell on him so that he cannot move another inch. A second later she disappears.) Oh dear, I'm stuck, I can't move anything.

MIRRORMAN   No - and you won't be able to until she releases you.

TOYMAN   How's she going to do that?

MIRRORMAN   You'll see. (Immediately STARLIGHT returns and frees him from the spell.)

TOYMAN   Dear, oh dear. I don't think I'll try that again.

(He returns to his seat.)

MIRRORMAN   (Chuckles.) Well, Starlight watched the box carefully and made quite sure that no water got into it and, at last, about two miles from the King's palace, the box stopped at a mill. The miller saw it, and took a long pole and drew it onto the shore. And he and his wife, were delighted when they saw the baby in it. They had no children of their own so they decided to look after it carefully as though it were their own son. Many years passed -

TOYMAN   How many?

MIRRORMAN   Many many.

TOYMAN   I see.

MIRRORMAN   And the boy grew up into a fine young man. Look, there he is working in the fields. *(He is there.)*

TOYMAN   What's he doing?

MIRRORMAN   What's it look like?

TOYMAN   Scything?

MIRRORMAN   That's right. Well, he was scything alone, when the King happened to come by -

TOYMAN   In disguise again?

MIRRORMAN   No, not in disguise. But the miller's son didn't know it was the King.

TOYMAN   Why not?

MIRRORMAN   Because he'd never seen him before.

TOYMAN   I see.

MIRRORMAN   Do you?

TOYMAN   I think so, yes.

MIRRORMAN   You will see if you look carefully. Ssh! Here is the King now.

(The KING enters to the miller's son. STARLIGHT watches and listens.)

KING   Good day, my man.

EDWARD   Good day, sir.

KING   Is this your land?

EDWARD Well, it's my father's, sir.

KING I see. What's your name?

EDWARD Edward, sir.

KING Edward, eh? That's a fine crop of wheat you're cutting.

EDWARD Yes, sir. It's been a good summer.

KING And so the miller is your father, eh?

EDWARD Yes, I suppose you could say so. I've always thought of him as father.

KING What do you mean? Either he is or he isn't.

EDWARD Well, you see, I'm not actually his son. I don't really know who my parents are. They discarded me, and the miller found me.

KING Found you?

EDWARD Yes sir.

KING Where?

EDWARD In a box. On the river.

KING In a box? On the river? When was this?

EDWARD Some years ago, sir. I was only a baby.

KING This is very interesting. Very interesting indeed. *(He moves away and talks to us.)* That must be the child I threw into the river. I can't have this. If he lives he will marry my daughter. I won't allow it.

EDWARD I beg your pardon, sir.

KING Nothing, I was talking to myself.

EDWARD Yes, sir.

KING Edward, do you know who I am?

EDWARD No, sir. You're a stranger to these parts. That I do know.

KING I am the King.

EDWARD Your Majesty! You will excuse me. I had no idea.

KING   That's all right, my boy. Would you do something for me?

(He starts to write on a piece of paper.)

EDWARD   With pleasure, your Majesty. Anything.

KING   Would you please take this message to the Palace and give it to the Queen?

EDWARD   I will, if you show me the way, your Majesty.

KING   Across the fields and over that hill, yonder. You will see the palace from the top of the hill. It's only two miles away.

EDWARD   I'll go at once, your Majesty.

KING   Thank you. Oh! The message is private, Edward.

EDWARD   You can depend on me your Majesty. I shall not read it.

(The KING goes. EDWARD tidies up the wheat and covers his scythe. Suddenly STARLIGHT is by his side.)

EDWARD   Hello! Are you here again?

STARLIGHT   You must be careful.

EDWARD   What d'you mean - careful?

STARLIGHT   I sense danger.

EDWARD   Danger! What nonsense. Now listen here, my friend. I don't know who you are and you won't tell me because you say it's a secret. Well - that's fine! And I don't deny you've been a great help to me. You pulled me out of the river when I fell in by mistake and was drowning - you killed the snake that would have killed me in the forest - you stopped my axe from cutting off my leg when the blade was loose without my knowing it. These, and many other things have you done for me. But really, you mustn't interfere. Now, I must hurry so that I'm home before sunset. Come if you like, but don't interfere.

STARLIGHT   I won't   *(They set off on their journey. They have gone only a little way when STARLIGHT says -)* This way.

EDWARD   That way? But that leads through the forest. It's much longer. The King said go over the hill.

STARLIGHT   Please don't. Please come this way. The hill is very dangerous. Please (*She brings him to a standstill by magic.*)

EDWARD   Oh, all right. But if we get lost, it's all *your* fault. (*Again they set off through the forest. And soon they do get lost.*) Now, which way?

STARLIGHT   (*Pointing.*) That way.

EDWARD   But we've just come that way.

STARLIGHT   That way.

EDWARD   But that's going towards the east. Oh dear, I knew we'd get lost in this forest. And now I'm tired out and can't walk much farther - and for all I know the palace is miles away. (*STARLIGHT gives a little contented laugh.*) And it's nothing to laugh about, either.

STARLIGHT   Look!

EDWARD   Where?

STARLIGHT   Over there. A light.

EDWARD   So it is. Perhaps there's a house. Yes, yes. Look. The light comes from a window. Come on, we'll go there and see if we can have a bed for the night. (*They move on and reach a cottage.*) There doesn't seem to be anyone about.

STARLIGHT   Knock!

(*EDWARD knocks.*)

EDWARD   Is there anyone there?

Enter an OLD WOMAN. As she does so, STARLIGHT hides.)

OLD WOMAN   Well, and what do you want?

EDWARD   I'm taking a letter to the Queen at the palace. But I've lost my way, and should be grateful if you would allow me to sleep here for the night.

OLD WOMAN   Indeed, young man. Well, as it happens, you're very unlucky. This hut belongs to some Robbers.

EDWARD   Robbers?

OLD WOMAN	Yes. And if, when they return, they find you here, it may be the worse for you.
EDWARD	Oh dear. What shall I do?
STARLIGHT	*(Off.)* Chance it!
OLD WOMAN	What was that?
EDWARD	Oh, nothing.
OLD WOMAN	Nothing, eh? Well, what d'you want to do. Go or stay?
EDWARD	I think I'll chance it. Anyway, I'm so tired I can go no farther tonight.
OLD WOMAN	As you will, young man. If you have no gold the robbers may leave you alone.
EDWARD	I have nothing at all, except the letter for the Queen.
OLD WOMAN	Keep that hidden on your person, then. You'd better sleep down here out of the way. Good night.
EDWARD	Good night. And thank you.

(He lies down to sleep. The woman goes.)

STARLIGHT	Where have you put the letter?
EDWARD	Why?
STARLIGHT	No reason.
EDWARD	Don't you worry. It's safe here in my shirt. Now you go and hide and have some sleep.
STARLIGHT	Good night.

(She hops away - but stays awake. EDWARD sleeps. The robbers arrive and at once they sense something is different. There can be any number of robbers, who can improvise their dialogue within the framework below.)

1ST ROBBER	Ssh! There's someone there!
2ND ROBBER	Where?
1ST ROBBER	Lying down there on the floor.
2ND ROBBER	What shall we do with him?

(Most of the remainder of this scene is improvised within the following framework -

1ST ROBBER is very anxious to cut EDWARD's throat.
2ND ROBBER is less anxious.

The robbers discuss together what should be done with him, and eventually resolve to kill him. Before they can do this, STARLIGHT wakes EDWARD and both run away. There is a chase. EDWARD and STARLIGHT are captured and brought back to the house.)

EDWARD	You can't kill me. You mustn't. I have to take a letter to the Palace for the King.
1ST ROBBER	For the King, eh? Well, we don't like the King.
2ND ROBBER	He makes too many laws in this land.
1ST ROBBER	Not that we care for his laws. The more he makes the more we break - but he'll hang us if he catches us.
2ND ROBBER	What is this letter?
EDWARD	I don't know what it's about. It's private, so I haven't read it.
1ST ROBBER	Haven't you? Well, we shall. Where is it?
EDWARD	Find it.
1ST ROBBER	We will find it. Search him, men. *(They search him and find the letter in his shirt pocket.)* Good work, men. Now, two of you take them both into the other room while we read it. *(EDWARD and STARLIGHT are taken into the other room.)* Sit down and I'll read it to you. *(He opens it and reads.)* "To Her Majesty the Queen - As soon as the man carrying this letter arrives, let him be put to death and immediately buried; let it be done before I return tomorrow morning. Signed - His Majesty the King."
2ND ROBBER	Looks as if the King would have done our work for us if we'd let the man alone.
1ST ROBBER	Ah! But perhaps this is a chance for us to get our revenge on the King! What shall we do with the letter?

(Another improvised discussion, the outcome of which is that they write another letter.)

2ND ROBBER	Listen, then. How's this? *(Reads.)* "To Her Majesty the Queen - As soon as the man carrying this letter arrives let him be married to our daughter, the Princess. Signed - His Majesty the King."
1ST ROBBER	I think we should kill him and have done with it.
2ND ROBBER	And be caught and hanged ourselves! You know perfectly well that if a King's messenger is killed the whole country searches until they find the murderers. We'd be bound to be caught. But this way, we get our revenge on the King, because he's very fussy about whom his daughter should marry.
1ST ROBBER	All right. Bring them back. *(EDWARD and STARLIGHT are brought back.)* You speak to them.
2ND ROBBER	We've decided to let you go, young man, now that we see how important is your letter to the Queen.
EDWARD	Thank you.
2ND ROBBER	Untie the ropes.
1ST ROBBER	Wait a minute. Why should we let them go without some reward. Let him bargain for his life. What can you give us in return for your freedom?
EDWARD	Nothing.
1ST ROBBER	Nothing?
EDWARD	I possess nothing.
1ST ROBBER	No gold?
EDWARD	Not a single piece.
1ST ROBBER	Well, you'd better think of something quickly or we shall change our minds. I'll give you up to five. One - two - three - four -
STARLIGHT	Give me to them.
2ND ROBBER	You? Who are you?
STARLIGHT	I'm - I'm his servant. I'm all he's got in the world. Really I am. And I could be very useful to you. I could sweep and cook and mend and darn - and look after you properly. Better than that old woman does.
1ST ROBBER	What do you say, men? *(They all agree.)* All right,

then. We'll take you in exchange for his life. Untie the ropes.

(*They do so.*)

STARLIGHT   May I have one moment to say good-bye to my master before he goes?

1ST ROBBER   I suppose so. I don't see any harm in that.

(*STARLIGHT draws EDWARD to one side.*)

STARLIGHT   (*Whispering.*) Don't worry. I'll play a trick on them and be with you in a minute or two (*Loudly.*) Good-bye, sir.

EDWARD   Good-bye.

1ST ROBBER   Get on your way, you.

(*EDWARD goes.*)

STARLIGHT   Now - what can I do for you?

2ND ROBBER   Yes, what can she do for us?

(*Another improvised discussion. It is suddenly interrupted by STARLIGHT calling out.*)

STARLIGHT   Look - down there. Something glistening! It's a diamond.

(*The ROBBERS all leap to see - and STARLIGHT runs.*)

1ST ROBBER   There's nothing there. Nothing at all. Where is she? We've been tricked. Come on, men. After her.

(*They run after her. But STARLIGHT puts a spell on them and leads them to a muddy swamp, where they all sink. This should take place off stage, as the robbers do not reappear. They should cry out about sinking in the mud. STARLIGHT rejoins EDWARD.*)

STARLIGHT   It's all right. They've sunk in the mud. It'll take them hours to get free.

EDWARD   I told you we should have gone across the hills. If we had, none of this would have happened.

STARLIGHT   But we had to go to the Robbers' den.

EDWARD   Why?

STARLIGHT   I can't tell you that. You'll find out one day. And look - here we are at the palace.

(Fanfare. Enter the QUEEN. EDWARD bows.)

EDWARD: Your Majesty. I am commanded by the King to deliver this letter to you.

(The QUEEN takes it and reads.)

QUEEN: Young man, do you know what this letter contains?

EDWARD: No, your Majesty. I haven't read it.

QUEEN: You are in luck, young man. For His Majesty tells me that you are to marry our daughter, the fairest girl in the land.

EDWARD: I am honoured, your Majesty.

QUEEN: *(Clapping her hands.)* Let all preparation be made for my daughter's wedding. The Royal Marriage shall take place this very day.

(Fanfare. Enter KING.)

KING: Stop! Stop! What is this? What do I hear - a Royal Marriage?

QUEEN: Yes, your Majesty. Welcome home to you. The young man you sent with the letter has only this moment arrived.

KING: Let me see the letter - *(He reads it.)* What have you done with the letter I gave you?

EDWARD: That is it, your Majesty.

KING: It is not.

EDWARD: But -

KING: Silence. I tell you this is not the letter. It has been changed.

EDWARD: Then it is not my fault sir. I was captured by some robbers who took the letter, read it and later returned it to me. I know nothing else about it.

KING: You shall not marry my daughter.

QUEEN: But my dear, he would make a very fine husband, and -

KING: No! No man shall marry my daughter who is not worthy of her.

QUEEN	But perhaps he is worthy, my dear.
KING	Then he must prove it.
EDWARD	How? How can I prove it? I will do anything your Majesty commands.
KING	Go then - go to the wonderful cave and bring me three golden hairs from the head of the giant who reigns there. Do this, and you shall have my consent.
EDWARD	Very well, your Majesty. I will do my best. I will go at once.

(He goes, followed by STARLIGHT.)

KING	*(To QUEEN.)* Come, my dear. We are well rid of him. No man who dared to go to the giant's cave has ever lived to tell the tale. Ha! Ha! *(They go.)*

(EDWARD and STARLIGHT journey onwards.)

EDWARD	Do *you* know the way to this cave?
STARLIGHT	Yes, I do. You have to go through a great city with two gates to go through and a lake to cross. And be careful when you reach each guard.
EDWARD	Careful?
STARLIGHT	Yes. These guards will each ask you a question. If you do not know the answers they won't let you pass.
EDWARD	Shall I know the answers?
STARLIGHT	I don't know.
EDWARD	Then what shall I do?
STARLIGHT	Tell them you'll give them the answer on your way home.
EDWARD	But shall I know them even then?
STARLIGHT	Wait. You'll see. Look. Here is the first gate of the city.

(The 1ST GUARD springs up.)

1ST GUARD	Halt! Who goes there?
EDWARD	A friend.

1ST GUARD	What friend? What is your business?
EDWARD	I wish to pass through your city to the Cave of the Giant King.
1ST GUARD	You may do so. But on one condition.
EDWARD	What is that?
1ST GUARD	Answer this question: "Why has the fountain in our market place dried up and will give no water?"
EDWARD	I - I don't know.
1ST GUARD	Then you cannot pass. Tell us, and not only will you pass through the City but we shall reward you with gold.
EDWARD	I - I -
STARLIGHT	Tell him you'll give him the answer on your way back.
EDWARD	I will give you the answer on my homeward journey.
1ST GUARD	Are you sure?
EDWARD	Certain.
1ST GUARD	Then pass. But make sure you do tell us when you return.
EDWARD	Thank you. *(They pass through the Gate.)* Are you sure I shall find out the answers?
STARLIGHT	Yes, yes, of course. I know you will.
EDWARD	But how?
STARLIGHT	Don't ask so many questions. Look, here we are at the second gate.

(The 2ND GUARD springs up.)

2ND GUARD	Halt! Who goes there?
EDWARD	A friend.
2ND GUARD	What friend? What is your business?
EDWARD	I wish to pass through your city to the Cave of the Giant King.
2ND GUARD	You cannot pass - unless you can answer one question.
EDWARD	I will try.
2ND GUARD	Tell us why a tree which used to bear us golden apples doesn't produce even a leaf?

EDWARD	I will tell you the answer when I return.
2ND GUARD	Are you sure?
EDWARD	Quite sure.
2ND GUARD	Then pass. But if you cannot tell us the answer you will be put to death.

(They go on through the city.)

EDWARD	I don't like this at all. We're taking an awful risk.
STARLIGHT	There's nothing to be afraid of.
EDWARD	That's all very well for you to say. I'm the one they'll put to death.
STARLIGHT	Ssh! Here we are at the great lake.
EDWARD	Who will take us across?
STARLIGHT	The guard. He is the ferryman too.

(The 3RD GUARD is present in his boat.)

3RD GUARD	Halt! Who goes there?
EDWARD	A friend.
3RD GUARD	What friend? What is your business?
EDWARD	I wish to cross your lake to the Cave of the Giant King.
3RD GUARD	Tell me but one thing and you shall cross.
EDWARD	I will try.
3RD GUARD	Why am I bound for ever to ferry people over this water? How can I get free, for I haven't stood on dry land for many, many years?
EDWARD	I will tell you all about it when I come home.
3RD GUARD	Are you certain?
EDWARD	Quite certain.
3RD GUARD	Then get into the boat and I will ferry you across the lake. *(They get into the boat and are taken over the lake.)* Look! There is the cave. I will wait for you to return.

(They leave the boat.)

STARLIGHT: Wait here. I'll see what the Giant King is doing.

(STARLIGHT creeps towards the cave. Enter an old lady with a large dish of fish which she places ready for the giant. STARLIGHT returns to EDWARD.)

STARLIGHT: The Giant King isn't here.

EDWARD: Isn't here?

STARLIGHT: No. But he'll be back at any moment - his lunch has been put ready for him.

EDWARD: Then what should we do?

STARLIGHT: Go into the cave. There you will see an old woman. She will ask if you know who she is. Tell her that you do know.

EDWARD: But I don't. Who is she?

STARLIGHT: The Giant King's Grandmother! Quickly, go, before the Giant returns.

(EDWARD goes into the cave.)

EDWARD: Er - good day!

WOMAN: Good day to you. Who are you?

EDWARD: My name is Edward. I am the miller's son.

WOMAN: What do you seek here?

EDWARD: Three golden hairs from the giant's head.

WOMAN: You are running a great risk, young man. If the giant finds you, he will kill you and eat you - as he has done many before.

EDWARD: But you could help me.

WOMAN: I could. And I shall - if you can tell me who I am.

EDWARD: I know who you are. You are the Giant King's Grandmother.

WOMAN: Quite right, young man, quite right. Then I will help you.

EDWARD: But I need other things besides the three golden hairs.

WOMAN   What things?

EDWARD   I need to know why the city fountain is dry, and why
                 the tree that bore golden apples is leafless, and
                 what it is that holds the ferryman to his boat.

WOMAN   Those are three very puzzling questions.

GIANT   (Off.)   What ho, grandmother!   Is my luncheon ready?

WOMAN   (Calling.) Yes, yes, my dear.   Quite ready.
                 (Whispering to EDWARD.)   Quickly, lie down here and
                 listen to what the giant says when I pull out the
                 golden hairs.

(She covers EDWARD with a blanket on the floor - only just in time.)

GIANT   (Entering.) I'm hungry. Very hungry. I could eat
                 a whole army of men.

WOMAN   I'm sorry, but there are no men to eat. You've
                 frightened them all away.

GIANT   (Sniffing.) All!   Are you sure?

WOMAN   Of course, my dear. No man has come to the cave for
                 many days.

GIANT   But I can small the flesh of man. Where is he?
                 Where is he?

WOMAN   Who, my dear?   There's no one here but ourselves.

GIANT   There is.   I know there is.   I can smell him. Come
                 out, wherever you are - I'll find you.   I'll find
                 you.

(He searches - and soon sees EDWARD quivering under the blanket. He raises his club to strike, but STARLIGHT puts a spell on him and helps EDWARD to another hiding place. Then STARLIGHT releases the giant.)

WOMAN   Come, sit down.   Sit down!   Why should you turn
                 everything topsy-turvey when I've spent all morning
                 putting it right?   Sit down at once, I say.

GIANT   Then give me my lunch at once.

WOMAN   Here it is.   All ready for you.   The finest and
                 largest fish from the lake.

GIANT   Pah! Fish! Ugh! (He eats it all in one gulp.)
                 There.   It's gone.   Is there any more?

WOMAN   I'm afraid not, my dear.

GIANT   Then I'll sleep first and go hunting afterwards.

WOMAN   That's right, my dear. Come and rest your head in my lap. *(He does so.)* There! Sleep well.

(The GIANT sleeps and snores. The WOMAN waits her chance and then pulls out a hair.)

GIANT   Ouch! Oh! What d'you think you're doing? Eh?

WOMAN   I'm sorry, my dear. I too fell asleep, and I was having a dream that disturbed me.

GIANT   What dream was that?

WOMAN   I dreamt that the fountain in the city market-place had dried up and would give no water. What on earth could be the cause?

GIANT   Huh! They'd be mightily pleased if they could find that out.

WOMAN   But of course nobody knows.

GIANT   What d'you mean - nobody knows? I know. I know everything. Let them look under a stone in the fountain; there sits a toad. A great fat toad. When they kill him, the water will flow again.

WOMAN   Thank you, my dear. I'm sure I won't dream that dream again.

GIANT   I hope you won't dream at all *(Again he sleeps and snores. Again the WOMAN waits her chance and pulls out a hair.)* Ouch! Oh! Can't you be more careful, woman? What do you think you are doing?

WOMAN   Oh, don't be angry, my dear. I did it in my sleep again.

GIANT   Another dream I suppose.

WOMAN   Yes, dear. I dreamt that a beautiful tree in the city that used to bear golden fruit now hasn't even a leaf on it. What could be the reason for that?

GIANT   Ah! Another secret they'd like to know. Well, if they looked at the foot of the tree they'd find a mouse, gnawing at the roots. If they kill the mouse, golden apples will grow again. But if they don't the tree will soon be dead. Now - leave me in peace. If you wake me again, I'll - I'll -

(He raises his club threateningly.)

WOMAN	Yes, dear. I know. Well, I promise you I'll try very hard not to.

(GIANT sleeps again and snores. The WOMAN again waits her moment and pulls out a hair.)

GIANT	Ouch! Oh, woman, I warned you! I'll eat you whole for pulling out my hair.
WOMAN	No! No! No, my dear. I really am very sorry. I dreamt yet again - a horrid dream.
GIANT	Away with your dreams.
WOMAN	Yes, dear. But really I can't help it.
GIANT	What was it about this time?
WOMAN	I dreamt I saw a ferryman who was forced to go backwards and forwards over a lake, and hadn't been on dry land for years.
GIANT	Tcha! Silly fool that he is. If he were to give the rudder to one of the passengers, he could get out of the boat and the passenger would have to take his place.
WOMAN	How very clever you are, my dear.
GIANT	Clever? Huh! I'm clever enough not to sleep with my head on your lap again. I'm going out into the forest.
WOMAN	Yes, dear. *(He goes.)* *(To EDWARD.)* Quickly, my friend. Take the hairs and hurry away from the cave before he should seek you.
EDWARD	Thank you. Thank you very much.
WOMAN	Quickly and quietly away you go. I'll see he doesn't come back.

(She goes one way - he another, to join STARLIGHT.)

STARLIGHT	Did you get them?
EDWARD	Yes, here they are.
STARLIGHT	Well done. Well done. Now the princess will be yours. The ferryman is still waiting for us.
3RD GUARD	Well - have you found out the answer to my question?
EDWARD	Take me across and then I'll tell you.

3RD GUARD	What's this? A trick?
EDWARD	No trick, my friend. As soon as we cross the lake I'll give you your answer.
3RD GUARD	Very well. But no nonsense, mind you. *(They cross the lake.)* Here we are then. Safely on the other side. Now, tell me how I can escape from this boat.
EDWARD	Why, give the rudder to one of the passengers, then run away as fast as you can and that passenger must take your place.
3RD GUARD	Ah! How simple. Yet I never thought of it myself.

(EDWARD and STARLIGHT run away laughing. They reach the second gate.)

2ND GUARD	Who is that?
EDWARD	'Tis I - with the answer to your question.
2ND GUARD	It had better be right, or I shall put you to death.
EDWARD	No. Don't kill me. Kill the mouse that gnaws at the root of the tree - then golden apples will grow again.
2ND GUARD	Ah! Thank you, sir. I must do it at once. *(He goes.)*

(EDWARD and STARLIGHT, laughing, continue with their journey. They reach the first gate.)

1ST GUARD	Who is that?
EDWARD	'Tis I, with the answer to your question.
1ST GUARD	If the answer's right, I shall load you with gold.
EDWARD	Then kill the toad that lies under a stone in the fountain. Then the water will flow again.
1ST GUARD	Thank you, my friend. Here, take the gold. It's as much as you or any man can carry.

(EDWARD picks up the sack of gold and with STARLIGHT continues the journey.

  Fanfare. The KING and QUEEN receive them.)

KING	So! You have returned, my boy, have you? The giant didn't kill you.

EDWARD No, your Majesty. And here are the three golden hairs from the head of the Giant King.

KING Am I then never to be rid of you? When you were a baby I heard that you were destined to marry my daughter and I bought you from your parents, put you into a box and threw you into the river -

EDWARD You did that?

KING Yes, I did. And then I dispatched you to the Queen with a letter commanding her to put you to death -

EDWARD So that was the letter you sent me with -

KING Yes, it was. Until you blundered into a band of robbers and had it stolen and altered. And now - now -

EDWARD You sent me to the Giant King expecting me to be eaten.

KING Exactly. You have a charmed life, my boy, and no mistake.

EDWARD I certainly have. For, so I am told, I was born under a lucky star. Good Heavens!

KING What?

EDWARD I've lost her!

KING Lost her? Whom have you lost?

EDWARD Well - the - the person! Starlight! That's who it was. The spirit from my lucky star. Oh dear. I do wish I hadn't lost her.

QUEEN Never mind, my son. You may have lost *her*. But surely you no longer have need of her. For now you have won our daughter. His Majesty cannot possibly refuse you now.

KING No, No. I shall not refuse him. He has indeed won the hand of the Princess. Look - here she is. *(Fanfare. Enter PRINCESS. EDWARD goes to her, and bows.)* Go, my children. And may you be happy for ever more.

EDWARD Thank you, sir.

KING Let the trumpets sound - and let music be played. For today we shall have a great ball to celebrate my daughter's wedding.

(Music. The Ball. After a while, the TOYMAN enters and the dancers melt away, leaving him alone.)

TOYMAN (To us.) Excuse me - we've been invited to the marriage feast, but we shan't stay very long - only about fifteen minutes.

(MUSIC. He goes.)

END ACT I

ACT 2

The TOYMAN enters, licking his fingers.

TOYMAN: Well, what a delicious feast that was. We had chicken and turkey and chips and peas - and jelly and fruit and ice-cream - and finally the largest cake you ever saw. It really was delicious.

(In suitable circumstances, and as an alternative, the above list can be left out and the audience be invited to suggest what the feast consisted of. The MIRRORMAN comes in, a little agitated.)

MIRRORMAN: Psst! You can't stay there.

TOYMAN: Oh, why not?

MIRRORMAN: What have you got in your hand?

TOYMAN: Only the nail.

MIRRORMAN: Only the nail? Well, you've been holding it so tightly that you've started the next story.

(The MIRRORMAN changes the "wall" into a window.)

TOYMAN: Have I really?

MIRRORMAN: Quickly - over here.

(They move away.)

THE ELVES AND THE SHOEMAKER

WIFE: *(Off.)* Go on! Out with you. Go and do an honest day's work.

(Enter the SHOEMAKER - followed first by one shoe and then another, both of which only just miss him.)

SHOEMAKER: Oh dear, oh dear, oh dear. I do wish she wouldn't carry on like that. She really is very nice, you know - my wife, I mean. But she does get so impatient.

WIFE: *(Entering.)* Haven't you gone yet? Hurry up, I say.

SHOEMAKER: My dear, please be reasonable. It's no good shouting at me to do a day's work. The only work I know anything about is shoemaking, and I haven't any leather to make shoes with, and I haven't any money to buy leather with. All we can do is to wait.

WIFE: Wait? What for, may I ask?

SHOEMAKER	A customer.
WIFE	A customer, indeed. You've nothing to sell.
SHOEMAKER	Oh yes I have, my dear. I have just one pair of shoes left. And they really are rather special.
WIFE	Then make sure you get a special price for them, that's all I can say.
SHOEMAKER	Yes, dear. *(He places the shoes in the shop-window.)*
WIFE	Don't go giving them away as you've done with nearly everything else we possessed.
SHOEMAKER	No, dear.
WIFE	Why, only the other day you gave away your overcoat. I saw you, so you needn't deny it.
SHOEMAKER	Well, dear, the old man was *very* cold. And I was quite warm here in the shop. Besides, I didn't really need the coat as I so seldom go out.
WIFE	Don't argue with me.
SHOEMAKER	No, dear.
WIFE	Goodness only knows how many people you've given away shoes to.
SHOEMAKER	Only to people who needed them, dear.
WIFE	Everybody needs them.
SHOEMAKER	Yes, dear. But not everybody can afford to buy them.
WIFE	No more can you afford to give them away.
SHOEMAKER	No, dear.
WIFE	Now just you sit there until you've sold the shoes.
SHOEMAKER	Yes, dear.
WIFE	And look sharp about it.
SHOEMAKER	Yes, dear.

(She goes off. The SHOEMAKER sits humming a song, rather mournfully. Presently there comes to him the KING OF THE ELVES, but the SHOEMAKER doesn't know who he is.)

KING	Good day, shoemaker.

SHOEMAKER   And a good day to you, sir. What can I do for you?

KING   I have a nail sticking into my foot. Can you knock it down for me, please?

SHOEMAKER   Certainly, sir.

(The KING takes off his shoe.)

KING   It's just in there. Can you see it - sticking out?

SHOEMAKER   Ah, yes, sir. I can see it.

KING   Can you mend it for me?

SHOEMAKER   Well - I can. But really, you know, these shoes are *past* repair. You ought to have some new ones.

KING   Do you really think so?

SHOEMAKER   I do indeed, sir. The damp has got into them and rotted the leather. They won't last many more days now.

KING   But I have no money to buy a new pair.

SHOEMAKER   Well, let's not worry about that for the present. First let me see if I've a pair that will fit you. *(He produces his only pair.)* What about these?

KING   They're very smart.

SHOEMAKER   They certainly are, sir. They're fit for a King. Now try them for size. *(The KING puts them on.)* How do they feel?

KING   Very well indeed. Yes. They're most comfortable, and they look extremely nice. What a shame I haven't any money.

SHOEMAKER   But they look so right on you. Anyone would believe they had been made specially for *your* feet. My, my, how nice it is to see a pair of shoes fit so well.

KING   Yes, my friend. But I tell you again - I haven't any money.

SHOEMAKER   Oh, don't worry about that. You can't possibly go walking round in those other old shoes - you'll catch a cold or rheumatism or something. You *need* a pair of shoes.

KING   Do you mean to say that you'll give me the shoes?

SHOEMAKER   With pleasure, sir. I can't believe they'd look as nice on anyone else - or fit as well, for that matter. If, of course, your fortunes change, and you find you have some money another day, and perhaps are passing the shop - then you could look in and pay something towards them. But I'll quite understand if you really can't manage.

KING   This is most, most generous of you! Very well. I will take them. Are you a rich man?

SHOEMAKER   Well, not exactly rich. But we have enough to live on - sometimes.

KING   Who knows? As a result of this act of kindness your fortunes may change.

SHOEMAKER   That's a very nice thought. Thank you, sir.

KING   No, thank *you*, my friend. Good day. I shall not forget you.

(As he goes, the WIFE comes back.)

WIFE   Well - have you sold them?

SHOEMAKER   Er - yes and no, dear.

WIFE   Yes and no dear? What talk is this?

SHOEMAKER   Well, you see, dear -

WIFE   Are you going to tell me you *gave* them away?

SHOEMAKER   Well, not quite that. You see, dear, the man really did need a new pair of shoes. I mean, look at his old ones.

WIFE   I don't want to see them. Take them away, or I'll throw them at you.

SHOEMAKER   Oh, don't be angry, dear. He looked a very honest gentleman. I'm sure he'll pay me back as soon as he has some money.

WIFE   I've heard quite enough. I'm going to bed.

SHOEMAKER   Yes, dear. So am I.

WIFE   And first thing in the morning you can go down to the market and try to earn some money. If you don't -

SHOEMAKER   Yes, dear. I'll try my very best, dear.

(They go. The shop is empty. After a moment or two the KING OF THE ELVES returns, this time with a large number of other elves.)

KING This is the shop. Quickly, come and sit down. *(They do so.)* Listen, and I'll tell you what happened. I was passing this shop earlier today when suddenly I felt a nail sticking into my foot. I asked the shoemaker to mend it - and he insisted that I have a new pair, even though I had no money with which to pay for them. Now the old man didn't know what I was King of the Elves. So I decided at that moment that we should reward him by doing something in return. What d'you think we can do that will help him?

(Improvised discussion, the outcome of which is that some collect leather and some collect nails, and then all make shoes as fast as they can, the whole night through. When morning comes -)

KING It's nearly morning. We must go away quickly so that they don't see us here. How many pairs have we done? How many? *(Repeats suggested number.)* Well, that is wonderful. Now he really will be able to earn his living. Quickly, away now, I can hear him coming.

(They go. Enter SHOEMAKER, yawning and stretching.)

SHOEMAKER Ooh! How early it is! Never mind. The market always starts early. If I can get there soon, maybe I can borrow some leather and nails and so make some new shoes to sell. *(He senses something unusual.)* That's funny. I'm sure that somebody has been in this room during the night. Did you see anybody? *(Suddenly he sees the shoes.)* Good gracious. Fancy that - one, two, three *(up to whatever number was made)* ...... pairs of shoes. Wherever did they come from? Are they mine? Can I sell them, do you think? *(The audience will answer these questions.)* How amazing! If I sell all these, we shall never be poor again. I'll sell them right away. *(He goes into audience.)* Shoes to sell! Shoes to sell! Who would like to buy a pair of shoes?

(Improvised selling of shoes to audience.)

How wonderful. I've sold them all. Now we really won't go hungry. I must tell my wife about this at once. It'll make her the happiest woman in the world - and perhaps she'll never be angry again. Good-bye - and thank you very much for buying them. *(He goes.)*

(The TOYMAN creeps forward, followed by the MIRRORMAN.)

TOYMAN   (*Whispering.*)   And what happened to his wife?   Did she stop grumbling?

MIRRORMAN   Oh, yes. She took to eating, instead. And she ate so much that she got round and fat and comfortable and spent every day happily eating and sleeping.

(*A gong sounds.*)

TOYMAN   What on earth was that?

MIRRORMAN   You did it.

TOYMAN   I did it?   (*The TOYMAN changes the "window" into another throne.*)

MIRRORMAN   Yes. I think you must be holding the feather in your hand.

TOYMAN   Yes, I am. But why should it cause a noise like that?

MIRRORMAN   Because you squeezed it - try it again and see.

(*The TOYMAN holds up his hand with the feather in it. Slowly he squeezes the feather - and again - Gong!*)

TOYMAN   Is the story starting?

MIRRORMAN   Very nearly. Hold the feather tightly - (*Gong*) - and keep hold until the music comes - (*Music - Chinese Music!*)

THE NIGHTINGALE

MIRRORMAN   That's it. That's it! Now - this story happened many years ago, in China, where all the people are Chinamen - and even the Emperor is a Chinaman (*Enter the EMPEROR.*)   a good, kind, wise Chinaman, who is very polite to everybody (*The EMPEROR bows.*) and spends much of his time sitting on his throne reading learned books.   (*The EMPEROR sits on the throne and reads.*)   And nearly always standing by the Emperor is his gentleman-in-waiting, the Lord Chancellor. (*Enter LORD CHANCELLOR.*)   He is called the gentleman-in-waiting because his main job is to stand by the Emperor and wait - and if anyone other than the Emperor speaks to him, he is so grand that he will only answer -

LORD CHANCELLOR   P!   (*Pronounced puh.*)

MIRRORMAN   The Emperor lived in a beautiful palace - the most beautiful in all China - (*Two PROPERTY MEN build the Palace around the EMPEROR and LORD CHANCELLOR.*) the palace was set in beautiful grounds, with lovely trees always in the bloom for Spring - *(Enter to one side 1ST PROPERTY MAN with branch of tree with blossoms.)* and beautiful flowers, some of them with little tinkling bells tied to them - *(Enter 2ND PROPERTY MAN with flowers with silver bells.)* the garden was so great that not even the gardener knew where it ended; and in one part of the garden was a great lake - *(The PROPERTY MEN put down their branches and flowers and fetch a lake, which they lay out carefully.)* and the lake was surrounded by flowers and trees. *(The PROPERTY MEN fetch their brances and flowers and surround the lake.)* And in these trees near to the lake, there lived a Nightingale - *(Enter NIGHTINGALE, flying to the lake.)* which sang so deliciously - *(The NIGHTINGALE sings.)* that all the people who heard it would say -

1ST PROPERTY MAN   How beautiful it is!

2ND PROPERTY MAN   How beautiful it is!

BOTH   This is better than anything else!

MIRRORMAN   People come from all over the world to hear the nightingale sing. Some of them wrote books about China, about the town, the palace, and the garden. But none of them forgot the nightingale - it was always put above everything else. These books went all over the world. And in the course of time some of them reached the Emperor. *(The PROPERTY MEN take away their branches and one of them returns with a book which he presents to the EMPEROR.)* The Emperor sat on his throne reading and reading, and nodding his head, very pleased to hear such beautiful descriptions of the town, the palace, and the garden. But every book ended with the same words -

EMPEROR   *(Reading.)* "Of all the beautiful things, the best of all is the Nightingale." What is this? The Nightingale? *(Reads again.)* "Of all the beautiful things, the best of all is the Nightingale." Why, I know nothing about a nightingale. Can it be possible that there is such a bird in my Kingdom - what's more, in my own garden - and I have never heard of it? Imagine my having to discover this from a book! Lord Chancellor!

LORD CHANCELLOR   Yes, your Imperial Majesty.

EMPEROR   There is said to be a very wonderful bird called a nightingale here in my garden. They say that it is better than anything else in all my great Kingdom. Why have I never been told anything about it?

LORD CHANCELLOR	I have never heard it mentioned, Imperial Majesty. It has never been presented at the Palace.
EMPEROR	I wish it to appear here this evening - to sing to me. The whole world knows what is in my garden, and I know nothing about it.
LORD CHANCELLOR	Your Imperial Majesty mustn't believe everything that is written in books. Books are often mere stories.
EMPEROR	But the book in which I read it was sent to me by the powerful Emperor of Japan, so it can't be untrue. I will hear this nightingale. I insist upon its being here tonight. I extend my most gracious invitation to it, and, if it is not forthcoming, I will have the whole court trampled on after supper.
LORD CHANCELLOR	I have never heard it mentioned before. But I will seek it and I will find it, your Imperial Majesty.

(Gong. Exit the EMPEROR. The LORD CHANCELLOR looks to the left and then to the right, but he cannot find the nightingale.)

LORD CHANCELLOR	Oh dear, what shall I do? If I cannot find the nightingale we shall all be trampled on after supper.

(Enter a COURTIER.)

COURTIER	Can I help you? You seem to have lost something or other?
LORD CHANCELLOR	P!
COURTIER	I beg your pardon. I asked if I could help you?
LORD CHANCELLOR	P!
COURTIER	Indeed. Rudeness will not help you.
LORD CHANCELLOR	Do you know who I am, sir?
COURTIER	No, I do not.
LORD CHANCELLOR	Then come a little closer and you may recognize me.

(The COURTIER moves closer.)

COURTIER	I beg your pardon, my Lord Chancellor. I really hadn't recognized you, or I shouldn't have dared to speak.
LORD CHANCELLOR	No person speaks to the Lord Chancellor unless addressed by him first.

COURTIER	I understand. And again I ask your pardon.
LORD CHANCELLOR	Granted this once. As you are a courtier the mistake is pardonable, but do not make it again.
COURTIER	No, my lord.
LORD CHANCELLOR	And perhaps you can help me. I am seeking the Nightingale.
COURTIER	The nightingale? What is that?
LORD CHANCELLOR	It is a bird.
COURTIER	A bird?
LORD CHANCELLOR	A bird that sings.
COURTIER	A bird that sings?
LORD CHANCELLOR	Kindly do not repeat everything that I say. It doesn't matter what the bird *does*. It is sufficient that its presence is commanded by His Imperial Majesty this very night. If I do not find it we shall all be trampled on.
COURTIER	Trampled on! My goodness, how fearful!
LORD CHANCELLOR	You have not heard this bird?
COURTIER	No.
LORD CHANCELLOR	Nor seen it?
COURTIER	Indeed, I haven't even heard tell of it before.
LORD CHANCELLOR	Then help me look.
COURTIER	Yes, your lordship.

(One looks to the right, the other to the left, but without success.)

BOTH	*(Meeting in the middle.)* Oh dear, what shall we do?

(Enter the KITCHEN MAID.)

LORD CHANCELLOR	Girl! Where are you going?
MAID	To my mother's, sir.
LORD CHANCELLOR	Where does she live, girl?

MAID	Down by the shore, sir. Through the wood.
LORD CHANCELLOR	Who are you?
MAID	A kitchen maid, sir. In the kitchen of his Imperial Majesty, the Emperor.
COURTIER	Have you every seen the nightingale?
LORD CHANCELLOR	*(To COURTIER.)* I am asking the questions.
COURTIER	I beg your pardon, my lord.
LORD CHANCELLOR	*(To MAID.)* Have you ever seen the nightingale?
MAID	Indeed I have. And heard it too.
LORD CHANCELLOR and COURTIER	Where?
MAID	Oh goodness, I know it very well. Each evening at this time, I am allowed to take food to my mother, who is ill. On my way back, when I'm tired, I rest for a while in the wood. And then I always hear the nightingale. Its song is the finest in all this land.
LORD CHANCELLOR	Girl! Listen to me. How would you like to be, instead of a maid - a - cook?
MAID	Indeed, sir, I should like that very much, sir.
LORD CHANCELLOR	And how would you like to see His Imperial Majesty the Emperor dining?
MAID	Indeed, sir, I should like that very much, too. I should be honoured.
LORD CHANCELLOR	Then take us at once to this nightingale. It is commanded to appear before his Imperial Majesty tonight.
MAID	I shall take you with great pleasure, sir. Kindly follow me.

(They set off on their journey. The KITCHEN MAID is followed by the LORD CHANCELLOR, who is followed by the COURTIER. Suddenly the COURTIER stops them.)

COURTIER	Listen! Listen! *(A cow is heard bellowing.)* There it is now. And I have never heard it before. Oh, what wonderful power for so small a creature.

(The KITCHEN MAID laughs.)

LORD CHANCELLOR   And why, girl, do you laugh?

MAID   Because, sir, that is not the singing of a nightingale - it is the bellowing of a cow. We have a long way to go yet.

LORD CHANCELLOR   His Imperial Majesty made no mention of a cow. Proceed.

(They go on as before. Presently the COURTIER stops again.)

COURTIER   Listen! Listen! There it is now. *(The croaking of frogs is heard.)* We have found it at last. How beautiful it is - like the tinkling of church bells.

MAID   *(Holding in her laughter.)* No, sir - that is the sound of frogs. But I think we shall soon hear it now.

LORD CHANCELLOR   Proceed then.

(Again they go on just as before. This time the MAID stops them.)

MAID   Listen! There it is now! Listen! *(They listen for a moment.)* And look - there is the bird itself. See - over there, among the branches.

LORD CHANCELLOR   Really? Can that possibly be it? I should never have thought it was like that. How common it looks. I suppose that seeing so grand a person as I has frightened all its colours away.

MAID   Ssh! You'll frighten the whole bird away if you aren't more careful. Ssh! *(She goes to the NIGHTINGALE.)* Little Nightingale! Our gracious Emperor wishes you to sing to him!

NIGHTINGALE   With the greatest of pleasure. Shall I sing now?

MAID   Oh! That is not the Emperor!

LORD CHANCELLOR   *(Clearing throat.)* Humph! Bird -

MAID   Oh, please, sir, you mustn't speak to it like that. You must address it with great politeness.

LORD CHANCELLOR   P! - Humph. My - my precious little Nightingale. I have the honour to command your attentance at court tonight, where you will charm his Gracious Majesty the Emperor with your fascinating singing.

NIGHTINGALE   It sounds best among the trees. But I shall willingly come if the Emperor really wishes it.

LORD CHANCELLOR	Thank you. Girl! Run before us. Say that we are bringing the nightingale.
MAID	I will. I will. *(She runs to the palace calling -)* The nightingale is coming. The nightingale is coming.

(Gong. Enter the EMPEROR.)

EMPEROR	What is that you say?
MAID	Your Imperial Majesty. The nightingale has been found and shall this minute arrive to obey your command that it should sing for you. See - they are coming now.

(Enter the LORD CHANCELLOR followed by the NIGHTINGALE and the COURTIER.)

LORD CHANCELLOR	Your Imperial Majesty. The nightingale.
EMPEROR	Welcome. Welcome to my Palace, honourable bird. From far and wide have I learned of your exquisite singing. But neither I nor my court have every heard you.
NIGHTINGALE	Shall I sing to you now?
EMPEROR	Please do.

(The NIGHTINGALE sings. All listen, enchanted, to the end of the song. When the song is over, everybody claps.)

EMPEROR	Most charming. Most charming. Now do I understand why so many should write books about your music. You shall be rewarded. You shall wear my golden slipper around your neck.
NIGHTINGALE	Thank you, Imperial Majesty. But I have had sufficient reward. I have seen tears in the eyes of the Emperor. And the tears of an Emperor have a wonderful power. God knows I am sufficiently rewarded.
EMPEROR	Then you shall have your own room in the palace with your own cage. And twice each day and once each night you shall be let out of the palace to fly where you will. And I, His Imperial Majesty the Emperor, appoint you Imperial Nightingale, Singer-in-Chief.

(Gong. The NIGHTINGALE is taken in procession to its Imperial Cage by the LORD CHANCELLOR, the COURTIER and the MAID. The EMPEROR sits on his throne and sleeps. When he is asleep the MAID goes to the NIGHTINGALE.)

MAID	Little Bird! Little Bird! *(The bird stirs.)* Ssh! Are you well? Are they treating you kindly?

NIGHTINGALE   Yes, as kindly as they understand.   I was happier
                     when I was free in the wood - but they don't
                     understand that.   I was happier when I could sing
                     when I pleased.   They don't understand that either.

MAID   Shall I let you fly free?

NIGHTINGALE   No.   For that would only hurt them.   If my singing
                     can bring tears to the Emperor's eyes, then I must
                     stay and sing for his pleasure.   Thank you for coming
                     to see me.

MAID   I must go to sleep now.   All the palace is asleep.
                     Tomorrow morning I'll come to see you again.   Goodnight.

(The MAID sleeps.   The NIGHTINGALE sleeps.   The palace sleeps.

Gong.   It is morning.   Enter the LORD CHANCELLOR.)

LORD CHANCELLOR   The sun shines again on your Imperial Majesty's
                     Kingdom.

EMPEROR   Good morrow, Lord Chancellor.   What pleasure or
                     business have we today?

LORD CHANCELLOR   Your Imperial Majesty's Parcel-carrier has brought to
                     the palace the largest parcel I ever saw.

EMPEROR   Which of my subjects has sent such a gift?

LORD CHANCELLOR   Not one of your subjects, Gracious Majesty.   The gift
                     is from His Imperial Highness, the Emperor of Japan.
                     The parcel is labelled "Nightingale."

EMPEROR   Nightingale!   Then the parcel will contain a gift of
                     books from the Emperor of Japan - books about the
                     exquisite singing of our own bird.   Let the books be
                     unwrapped and brought to me at once.

LORD CHANCELLOR   Yes, gracious Majesty.   *(He goes, bowing. But in a
                     moment he returns.)*

LORD CHANCELLOR   Imperial Majesty!   Imperial Majesty!   Your Lord
                     Chancellor has made a mistake.   Your pardon,
                     gracious Majesty.

EMPEROR   What mistake has the Lord Chancellor made?

LORD CHANCELLOR   The parcel brought by the Imperial parcel-carrier from
                     his Imperial Highness the Emperor of Japan does not
                     contain books -

EMPEROR   Then what does it contain?

LORD CHANCELLOR	*A Nightingale*, gracious Majesty!
EMPEROR	A nightingale!
LORD CHANCELLOR	Yes, gracious Majesty. And tied by a ribbon to its neck - this note.
EMPEROR	*(Reading.)* "The Emperor of Japan's nightingale is very poor compared to the Emperor of China's." What nightingale is this?
LORD CHANCELLOR	An artificial nightingale, Imperial Majesty. A clockwork nightingale.
EMPEROR	Let it be brought into my presence.

(The LORD CHANCELLOR goes, and returns with the COURTIER, carrying the artificial nightingale. They set it down.)

EMPEROR	Why, it is beautiful - more beautiful even than the one in my garden. Can it be made to sing?
COURTIER	Yes, your Imperial Majesty. By winding it up.
EMPEROR	Then let it be wound up so that I may hear it sing.

(The bird is wound up - and sings - but only a waltz. One waltz. While it is singing, the real nightingale flies away.)

EMPEROR	How amazing! Astonishing! Lord Chancellor! Let a thousand messengers carry our gracious thanks to the powerful Emperor of Japan. Let it be done at once.
LORD CHANCELLOR	Yes, your Imperial Majesty. *(He goes.)*
COURTIER	Imperial Majesty, have you noticed how much more beautiful this bird is than the other? It is so studded with diamonds that it glistens like the finest bracelets and breast-pins in your gracious Majesty's Kingdom.
EMPEROR	It is indeed very pretty. Go and fetch me the other bird. We shall compare them side by side and hear them sing together.
COURTIER	Yes, gracious Majesty. At once, gracious Majesty.

(He goes. At once he and the LORD CHANCELLOR return.)

COURTIER	Gracious Majesty, a terrible thing has happened.
LORD CHANCELLOR	The bird is not there, your Highness. The bird has flown away.
EMPEROR	What? What is the meaning of this?

COURTIER	I do not know, gracious Majesty.
LORD CHANCELLOR	The wretched bird was jealous, no doubt. We are well rid of it, your Highness. An ill-mannered bird!
COURTIER	An ungrateful bird!
LORD CHANCELLOR	After all your Majesty has done for it.
COURTIER	To fly away without a word. Indeed your Majesty is well rid of it.
LORD CHANCELLOR	And, as you can see, your Imperial Majesty has yet the best bird of all.
EMPEROR	The best?
LORD CHANCELLOR	Indeed, gracious Majesty. With the real nightingale, you never knew what you would hear. But in the clockwork one everything is decided beforehand.
COURTIER	So it is, and so it must remain.
LORD CHANCELLOR	It cannot be otherwise, gracious Highness. See! You can look inside and see how it works. How each note follows on another to make up the song that it sings.
COURTIER	And because it sings only the one song, that song will become famous throughout your Kingdom, and will be sung by all your subjects.
EMPEROR	We are convinced. This is the best bird to have. Banish the real nightingale from our Kingdom.

(Gong. The LORD CHANCELLOR, EMPEROR and COURTIER freeze on the spot.

Enter from another part of the palace, the KITCHEN MAID.)

MAID	So they've banished the real nightingale out of the Kingdom. And now they all prefer the clockwork one. Well, it is very nice, I must admit; but there is something missing in it; I can't say quite what it is, but it doesn't seem to have a heart. Oh dear. How sad I am. I just cannot rest until I find the real one. *(Calls.)* Nightingale! Little Bird! Nightingale! - *(She goes.)*

(Gong. And the three stately people unfreeze again - and suddenly, there is just the smallest touch of unbending among them.)

EMPEROR   Let us wind it up again.

LORD CHANCELLOR   Yes. Let's. And let's see it dance as well as sing.

(They wind it up. It begins to sing the same waltz. After a while the COURTIER begins to hum the tune, then the LORD CHANCELLOR - then the EMPEROR, until eventually they are all dancing and humming the tune with the bird. After a while, the bird begins to run down, in the manner of a clockwork toy.)

EMPEROR   Lord Chancellor! What is the matter?

LORD CHANCELLOR   I really don't know, your Imperial Majesty.

COURTIER   It's quite all right, your Highness. It's just running down. We can soon put that right again. All you need do is to wind it again.

(The LORD CHANCELLOR winds it up, and again they hum and sing and dance - until suddenly - WHIZZ - then - WHIRR - BANG - and the nightingale stops.)

EMPEROR   Send for the doctor, quickly; something dreadful's happened.

COURTIER   A doctor won't do, your Imperial Majesty. What would he know of clockwork things? Far better to send for the watchmaker.

LORD CHANCELLOR   P!

EMPEROR   He is quite right, Lord Chancellor. Send at once for the Imperial Watchmaker-in-Chief.

LORD CHANCELLOR   Sir! Go at once. Summon the Imperial Watchmaker-in-Chief to the presence of the Emperor.

COURTIER   *(A little sourly.)* Yes, Lord Chancellor! *(He goes.)*

EMPEROR   Really, my Lord Chancellor. This is your fault.

LORD CHANCELLOR   If you say so, your Imperial Majesty, then it must be so. I deserve to be trampled upon. *(He prostrates himself.)*

EMPEROR   And you shall be - *(Putting his foot on the CHANCELLOR's neck.)*

LORD CHANCELLOR   Thank you, your Imperial Majesty.

EMPEROR   Unless the watchmaker can mend it again.

(Enter COURTIER and WATCHMAKER.)

WATCHMAKER	You summoned me, gracious Majesty?
EMPEROR	Indeed I did.
WATCHMAKER	In what way can I serve you? Is it a watch or a cuckoo-clock?
EMPEROR	Neither. It is a nightingale.
WATCHMAKER	A nightingale! Then I cannot help you, your Highness.
LORD CHANCELLOR	P!
EMPEROR	But surely a clockmaker and mender can mend or make a clockwork nightingale?
WATCHMAKER	I can try, your Imperial Highness.
LORD CHANCELLOR	Then do so. Don't stand talking. There is the bird.

(The WATCHMAKER falls to examining it.)

WATCHMAKER	Let me see, now. Let me see, let me see.

(He goes round and gazes at it with much hammering and tutting, tapping and searching.)

EMPEROR	Well? Can something be done?
WATCHMAKER	It really is very difficult, Imperial Majesty. I don't know that I can do it.
EMPEROR	Then I shall have you trampled upon and find a watchmaker who *can* mend it.
WATCHMAKER	Patience, gracious Majesty, patience, I beg of you. I am doing my best. *(Again he examines it. And suddenly says -)* Ahhh!
LORD CHANCELLOR	You have found the fault?
COURTIER	You know what's wrong?
EMPEROR	You can mend it soon?
WATCHMAKER	I think I can, gracious Majesty. *(Searches.)* It's the spring.
ALL THREE	The spring!

WATCHMAKER	Yes, it's broken.
ALL THREE	Then mend it –
LORD CHANCELLOR	Quickly –
COURTIER	As far as you can –
EMPEROR	And I shall give you a large reward.
WATCHMAKER	Thank you. Thank you, gracious Majesty.

(He bows and scrapes, and then goes back to the job. He pulls out the end of a spring.)

WATCHMAKER	*(To LORD CHANCELLOR.)* Would you please hold this?
LORD CHANCELLOR	P!
EMPEROR	Lord Chancellor, kindly hold it.
LORD CHANCELLOR	Of course, of course, Imperial Majesty. *(He holds it disdainfully.)* I am holding it.
WATCHMAKER	Thank you. Now pull.
LORD CHANCELLOR	Pull?
WATCHMAKER	If you would be so kind, Lord Chancellor.
LORD CHANCELLOR	P!
EMPEROR	*(With a great Imperial voice.)* PULL!
LORD CHANCELLOR	Of course, gracious Majesty, of course.

(He pulls. From the clockwork nightingale come some yards of mainspring.)

WATCHMAKER	Now, we're nearly there. Hold very tight, if you would be so kind. *(He slowly coils up the yards of spring, thoroughly tying-up everyone in his anxiety. Eventually it is done.)* And now, gracious Majesty, if only I can make this stay in place, the bird should sing again. *(He works hard.)* There! It's done! Oh, no. No it's not. There's a note out of place. That won't do. It will never do at all. There – we – are – now! It is done, your Imperial Majesty.
EMPEROR	Kindly receive our thanks, Imperial Watchmaker-in-Chief. A reward will be brought to your house this very day.
WATCHMAKER	Thank you, gracious Majesty.

LORD CHANCELLOR	Wind up the Bird, then!
WATCHMAKER	Oh no! No, I mustn't do that, Lord Chancellor.
LORD CHANCELLOR	P! Why not?
EMPEROR	Yes, why not indeed?
WATCHMAKER	Because, gracious Majesty, the bird has been overworked already. If you wind it again so soon, it may never work again.
EMPEROR	When can we wind it them?
WATCHMAKER	Imperial Majesty, I regret to tell you that it would be unwise to - to -
LORD CHANCELLOR	To what?
WATCHMAKER	To wind it more than once a year!
ALL THREE	What?
WATCHMAKER	My humble regrets, gracious Majesty. That is the best advice I can give, even though it means I may have to be trampled upon!
EMPEROR	Then take the bird away and mend it properly, so that I can wind it up whenever I choose. *(Exit WATCHMAKER with Bird.)* Lord Chancellor, send for my private physician.
LORD CHANCELLOR	Your doctor, Imperial Highness?
EMPEROR	Yes, yes. Make haste. For I feel very ill.
LORD CHANCELLOR	*(To Courtier.)* Go at once for the Imperial Physician-in-Chief. Tell him his gracious Highness is ill. *(COURTIER goes.)* Come, your Imperial Highness. Lie down here and rest till the doctor comes. *(With great difficulty he helps the EMPEROR to lie down.)*
EMPEROR	*(During this.)* I feel helpless and weak. Help me down, Lord Chancellor. *(He lies down and rests.)*

(Gong. Enter the DOCTOR with COURTIER.)

DOCTOR	You summoned me, Imperial Majesty.
LORD CHANCELLOR	He cannot speak. He is ill. Attend to him at once.

(DOCTOR attends. Silence.)

DOCTOR: I don't know what we can do. He is ill with a great sadness.

LORD CHANCELLOR: Will his Imperial Majesty get well again?

DOCTOR: I cannot tell. I will do my best. But I fear he may be dying.

(Gong. They all freeze, the DOCTOR attending the EMPEROR, the others looking on.
In the garden is the KITCHEN MAID.)

MAID: I don't know where our bird has gone. I have searched and searched everywhere and cannot find her. And now our Imperial Emperor, the great, good and kind Imperial Emperor, is ill with a great sadness. And I think it is sadness at the loss of his real nightingale - the best thing in all his Kingdom. And if I don't find her, I'm afraid he will die. Oh where, where can she be? Perhaps if I stay here by the lake she will come back to me. *(She kneels by the lake.)*

(Gong. The group unfreezes. The DOCTOR stands up.)

DOCTOR: Let us leave him in peace, so that he can rest.

LORD CHANCELLOR: Let no one stir, lest they disturb the sleep of his Imperial Majesty. Come. *(They go away, quietly.)*

MAID: I know! Perhaps if we all wished very hard she would return to us. Shall we try it? Shall we? Good. Then close your eyes, and wish - and wish - and wish. *(The NIGHTINGALE is heard in the distance.)* Listen! There she is now. Can you hear her? Nightingale. Little bird! Nightingale! *(The NIGHTINGALE flies in.)* Oh, welcome, little Nightingale. Where have you been all this time?

NIGHTINGALE: I've been in hiding, so that the Emperor wouldn't know that I hadn't left his Kingdom.

MAID: Oh, he'll be so glad that you haven't left. He needs you so very badly.

NIGHTINGALE: Needs me?

MAID: Yes. The clockwork nightingale has broken down and his Imperial Majesty is ill with a great sadness. Some think that he's said because of the clockwork bird, but I think it's because he banished you! Would you please go to him and sing? Please!

NIGHTINGALE	If he is sad, then yes, of course I will. I'll sing until he loses his great sadness.
MAID	Thank you. Thank you. I knew you would.

(The NIGHTINGALE flies into the palace, and standing close to the EMPEROR's bed, sings her beautiful song. Soon the EMPEROR wakes.)

EMPEROR	Oh, little bird! I hoped that you would return. I banished you from my Kingdom and yet you have charmed away sadness with the beauty of your song. How can I ever repay you?
NIGHTINGALE	You have rewarded me. I shall never forget that the first time I sang to you, I brought tears to your eyes. Those tears are the jewels which gladden the heart of a singer. I shall never ask for more.
EMPEROR	You must always stay with me. You shall sing only when you like, and I will break the clockwork bird into a thousand pieces.
NIGHTINGALE	Don't do that, gracious Emperor. It did all the good it was able. Keep it as you've always done.
EMPEROR	I shall, as you ask it. But will you come and stay with me?
NIGHTINGALE	I cannot build my nest and live in this palace, but let me come when I like, then I will sit on the branch in the evening and sing to you. I will sing to cheer you, and to make you thoughtful, too. I will sing to you of the happy ones, and of those who suffer too. I will sing about the good and evil, which are kept hidden from you. The little singing bird flies far and wide, to the poor fisherman and the peasant's home, so many who are far from you and your court. I love your heart more than your crown, so I will come, always I will come, and sing to you.
EMPEROR	Thank you. Thank you little bird. *(He sits up.)*
NIGHTINGALE	But you must promise me one thing.
EMPEROR	Everything!
NIGHTINGALE	*One* thing I ask of you. Tell no one that you have a little bird who tells you everything. It will be better so.
EMPEROR	I promise.

NIGHTINGALE	I hear people coming. Must fly away. Good-bye, Gracious Emperor. *(She flies away.)*
EMPEROR	Good-bye, Nightingale. *(He stretches out his hand.)* Why, fancy - she's dropped a feather. I shall keep it always. I hear people coming. I'll pretend to be ill again.

(Voices become louder. The EMPEROR lies down.)

LORD CHANCELLOR	*(To COURTIER as he enters.)* I'm afraid we shall find that his Imperial Majesty has died.
COURTIER	And we shall have to appoint a new Emperor -
LORD CHANCELLOR	Me!
COURTIER	P!

(They reach the bedside.)

LORD CHANCELLOR	Ssh!
COURTIER	Ssh!

(Suddenly the EMPEROR leaps up and says.-)

EMPEROR	Good morning! A very good morning to all of you. *(Gong. LORD CHANCELLOR and COURTIER prostrate themselves.)* And Lord Chancellor, if ever again I hear you say you shall be Emperor, I shall have you trampled upon - after supper.

(Gong. They freeze. When they are still the MIRRORMAN continues his story.)

MIRRORMAN	And so the Emperor, the good, kind, wise Emperor, recovered from his great sadness and lived to a great age. And he became the most famous of all the Emperors of China.

(Music. As he goes on with his story, the group unfreezes, the EMPEROR, the LORD CHANCELLOR and the COURTIER go out in procession and the PROPERTY MEN return to take away the lake, the trees and the palace. By the time the MIRRORMAN finishes his story the Toyshop has returned to its usual state.)

> Sometimes he left his beautiful palace and the lovely trees always in the bloom of spring, left the great lake and the beautiful flowers with little tinkling bells tied to them and went on a long journey. But though he visited all parts of his kingdom and saw many wonderful things, he always kept his promise to

the nightingale and never told anyone of the little bird who sang to him each evening - the most wonderful thing of all.

(As he ends the story the TOYMAN returns, sees one of the NIGHTINGALE's feathers, picks it up and holds it in his hand.)

TOYMAN	*(Quietly to himself.)* Good-bye, little Nightingale. I shall remember you for ever.
MIRRORMAN	Come along. Quickly. You'll have to hurry, you know, if you're to get that present to the Princess in time.
TOYMAN	My word, I shall have to hurry. *(They arrive at the mirror.)*
MIRRORMAN	Quickly - back through the mirror you go.
TOYMAN	Just a minute. What about the gentle hum?
MIRRORMAN	Don't worry about that. It'll come as soon as you put your hands flat against the mirror.
TOYMAN	Thank you for showing me the stories. The Princess is sure to be pleased.
MIRRORMAN	I hope she will. By the way - if ever you're stuck for a story, just pick up something you see - hold it tightly in your hand and think very hard - you're bound to think of something.
TOYMAN	What a good idea. I'll try that. I really will.
MIRRORMAN	Now - through you go.

(The TOYMAN puts his hands flat against the mirror. He has the musical box under his arm. The humming starts and he begins to come through.)

TOYMAN	I'm going through. Good-bye, Mirrorman, and thank you very much.
MIRRORMAN	Not at all - good-bye!

(The TOYMAN comes through. At once the MIRRORMAN becomes a reflection again. The TOYMAN, just in front of the mirror, but with his back to it, opens the musical box, and the music starts. He puts the objects into it.)

TOYMAN	A pea! Three golden hairs! A nail! And the feather.

(He leaves the box open so that the music still plays. Then he turns his face to the mirror, smiles, gives a little wink and moves away till his reflection disappears.)

TOYMAN *(To us.)* I must hurry to the palace with my present. Good-bye! And thank you for helping.

(And with the musical box still playing, he sets off for the palace.

Soon we cannot hear the music at all. The TOYMAN has gone.)

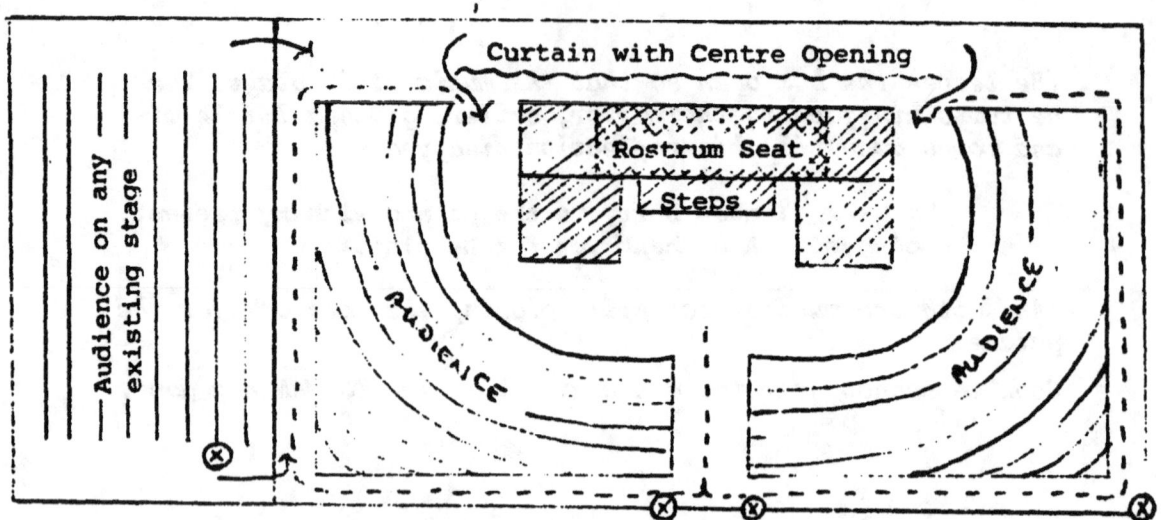

Long arrows indicate possible entrances. Single shading-line indicates one level of rostrum blocks; double shading indicates higher level. Dotted line indicates gangways necessary for processions and chases.

Lighting. Three or four spots (Marked X) will cover the acting area adequately. (House Lights may be added for processions and chases.)

The Curtain and rostrum block setting designed by the author for the London Children's Theatre Company's production of *The Storytellers*.

The "mirror" consists of a simple frame. This can be adapted for each story in the play by hanging different curtains or drapes at the back of the frame.

Props

All indicated in the script are necessary, except for those involving audience participation - e.g. the twenty mattresses and twenty feather beds in "The Real Princess" and the shoes in "The Elves and the Shoemaker."

Music

Indications are made in the script where music is necessary as a link between scenes or as an enrichment to certain parts of the action.

Suitable music will be found in the following -

       "Marching Strings"   (Ray Martin).
       "Wedding Fanfares"   (Bliss).
       "Waltzing Cat"   (Ray Martin).
       "L'Apprenti Sorcier" (Dukas).

and any suitable eastern music obtainable.

In "The Nightingale" the actors who take the parts of the two birds should make up their own tunes. That of the artificial nightingale should be sung with a metallic tone.

Audience Participation

The participation of the audience changes the play for them from one to look at to one they share in. This participation should be taken seriously by the actors (particularly by adults playing to children) and great care taken not to come out of character nor to behave as though in a slapstick pantomime. Suggestions by the audience should be taken at their face value, considered, and everything done to incorporate them in the production.

Practice in improvisation can best help the actor to be flexible and spontaneously creative; sensitively to avoid getting in anyone's way; to move swiftly down gangways; to be ready to hear clearly softly spoken words; and quickly and easily to make necessary changes.

The audience is referred to as "us" in order to emphasize the part given to them.

SPECIAL NOTE
Audience Participation, the text by the master--Brian Way--is now available from Baker's Plays, 100 Chauncy St., Boston MA 02111.

AUDIENCE PARTICIPATION
Theatre for Young People
by Brian Way

An in-depth text, compelling and authoritative, detailing discoveries the author has made in over 30 years of writing, acting, directing and designing. Contains practical approaches to audience participation in the open stage and proscenium theatres, breakdown of age groups and size of audience, economics and participatory theatre, integration with other arts and media, acting for children's theatre, open stage and teen-age production, technical theatre for the young audience production, mirror excercises and tips on vocal training. "His commitment to children's theatre and his innovative methods have made Brian Way one of the most important leaders in the field today. *Audience Participation* is rich in detail... the text we've been waiting for and it doesn't disappoint us." – Nellie McCaslin, Past President CTA, author of *Creative Dramatics in the Classroom*.

Here is Brian Way on such subjects as:
Audience Participation : "...the basis of the phenomenon of audience participation as a natural vocal and physical expression is of the heart, the mind and the spirit."

Performance Space : "Where does the action take place? The answer is – *everywhere*. The stage and the auditorium need to be thought of as one, not as comprising one place for the actors and another for viewers. A space in which anything can happen."

Performance : "Magic of the kind I am thinking of in Children's Theatre, with or without active participation of the audience, has little to do with the mind, but is a thing of the heart and the feelings and the spirit. Perhaps it is a syntheses of all man's different capabilities."

Random Thoughts : "The fascinating factor of theatre is that it can include so much 'stretching of experience,' so many fascinating things to think about at the time and ponder later and so many pictures to stimulate 'wonder' rather than diagram to solidify 'knowledge.'"
"Expression is a vital balance in a world that is more and more filled with impression."
"Only school and erroneous moments of correction in the home cause the birth of fear of failure."

Brian Way is referred to by many as "the most innovative children's theatre playwright in the English speaking language." He has written over 50 plays – 32 published by Baker's, was co-founder of Theatre Centre, London and its director for 25 years, author of the most popular text in the field today, *Development Through Drama*, professional director and instructor in acting at professional drama schools. He is now devoting his time exclusively to teaching, directing and conducting his highly praised workshops.

BAKERSPLAYS.COM

www.ingramcontent.com/pod-product-compliance
Lightning Source LLC
Chambersburg PA
CBHW051215290426
44109CB00021B/2460